MY FIRST

ICELAND

ALL ABOUT ICELAND FOR KIDS

GL⊕BED

CHILDREN BOOKS

Interior and cover Design: Daniel Day
Editor: Margaret Bam

For My Sons, Daniel, David and Jude

Blue Lagoon, Iceland

Iceland

Iceland is a **country**.

A country is land that is controlled by a **single government**. Countries are also called **nations, states, or nation-states**.

Countries can be **different sizes**. Some countries are big and others are small.

Hallgrimskirkja Cathedral, Reykjavík

Where Is Iceland?

Iceland is located in the continent of Europe.

A continent is a massive area of land that is separated from others by water or other natural features.

Iceland is situated in the North Atlantic Ocean and in the Arctic Ocean.

Reykjavík, Iceland

Capital

The capital of Iceland is Reykjavík.

Reykjavík is located in the **southwestern part** of the country.

Reykjavík is the largest city in Iceland.

Vik, Iceland

Counties

Iceland is a country that is made up of 23 counties

The counties of Iceland are as follows:

Reykjavík, Keflavík, Garður, Sandgerði, Vogar, Stykkishólmur, Grundarfjörður, Ólafsvík, Snæfellsbær, Borgarnes, Akranes, Ísafjörður, Bolungarvík, Súðavík, Patreksfjörður, Sauðárkrókur, Skagaströnd, Húnaþing vestra, Akureyri, Hörgársveit, Fjallabyggð, Skútustaðahreppur and Egilsstaðir.

Family in Iceland

Population

Iceland has population of around **300,000 people** making it the 171st most populated country in the world and the 39th most populated country in Europe.

Size

Iceland is **102,775 square kilometres** making it the 17th largest country in Europe by area.

Iceland is the 106th largest country in the world.

Languages

The official language of Iceland is Icelandic which is a North Germanic language. Almost all Icelandic people speak Icelandic as their first language.

English is widely spoken in Iceland, and it is often used as a second language in schools and workplaces. Danish, German, French, and Spanish are also spoken in Iceland.

Here are a few Icelandic phrases
- Vinsamlegast - Please
- Góðan daginn - Good morning

Þingvellir National Park

Attractions

There are lots of interesting places to see in Iceland.

Some beautiful places to visit in Iceland are

- Blue Lagoon
- Þingvellir National Park
- Hallgrímskirkja
- Gullfoss Falls
- Jökulsárlón
- Skógafoss

Skogafoss Waterfall, Iceland

History of Iceland

People have lived in Iceland for a very long time, in fact Iceland was first settled by Norse and Celtic people in the late 9th and early 10th centuries.

In 1380, Iceland became part of the Kalmar Union, a political union between Denmark, Norway, and Sweden.

In 1944, Iceland declared full independence from Denmark and became a republic.

Akureyri, Iceland

Customs in Iceland

Iceland has many fascinating customs and traditions.

- Icelanders have a tradition of eating fermented shark, which is considered a delicacy.
- Icelanders celebrate the summer solstice on June 21st with a festival called Jónsmessa. They light bonfires, sing songs, and tell stories.
- Swimming is a popular sport in Iceland and almost every town has a swimming pool.

Woman in Iceland

Music of Iceland

There are many different music genres in Iceland such as Pop, Rock, Classical, Folk and Electronic.

Some notable Iceland musicians include
- Of Monsters and Men
- Björk
- Sóley
- Sigur Rós
- GusGus
- Emilíana Torrini

Hákarl

Food of Iceland

Iceland is known for having delicious, flavoursome and rich dishes.

The national dish of Iceland is **Hákarl** which is a delicacy made from cured shark flesh.

Food of Iceland

Some popular dishes in Iceland include

- **Plokkfiskur – Fish Stew**
- **Hangikjöt – Smoked Lamb**
- **Harðfiskur – Dried Fish**
- **Rúgbrauð – Hot Spring Rye**
- **Kjötsúpa - Lamb Soup**
- **Pylsur - Lamb Hot Dog**
- **Langoustines - Lobster**

Reykjavik, Iceland

Weather in Iceland

Iceland has a **subarctic climate**, which is characterized by mild summers and cold winters.

Iceland's weather can be unpredictable. Due to its location in the North Atlantic, the country experiences frequent weather changes and strong winds.

Icelandic horse

Animals of Iceland

There are many wonderful animals in Iceland.

Here are some animals that live in Iceland

- Puffins
- Icelandic horse
- Icelandic Sheepdog
- Icelandic sheep
- Atlantic puffin
- Harbor seal
- Grey seal

Hvannadalshnúkur

Mountains

There are many beautiful mountains in Iceland which is one of the reasons why so many people visit this beautiful country every year.

Here are some of Iceland's mountains

- Hvannadalshnúkur
- Kirkjufell
- Snæfellsjökull
- Vestrahorn
- Eyjafjallajökull

German football fan

Sports of Iceland

Sports play an integral part in Icelandic culture. The most popular sport is Football.

Here are some of famous sportspeople from Iceland

- Eiður Guðjohnsen- Football
- Gunnar Nelson - MMA
- Ragnheiður Ragnarsdóttir - Swimming
- Alfreð Finnbogason - Football

Iceland Football Fan

Famous

Many successful people hail from Iceland.

Here are some notable Icelandic figures

- **Magnús Ver Magnússon - Strongest Man**
- **Björk - Singer**
- **Halldór Laxness - Novelist**
- **Bjarni Tryggvason - Astronaut**

Kirkjufell Mountain, Iceland

Something Extra...

As a little something extra, we are going to share some lesser known facts about Iceland.

- Iceland is the most sparsely populated country in Europe.
- Iceland is home to the world's oldest parliament, the Althing, which was established in 930 AD.
- Icelanders have a tradition of eating fermented shark, which is considered a delicacy.

Words From the Author

We hope that you enjoyed learning about the wonderful country of Iceland.

Iceland is a country rich in culture and beauty, with lots of wonderful places to visit and people to meet.

We hope you continue to learn more about this wonderful nation. If you enjoyed this book, consider leaving a review!

With Love

Printed in Great Britain
by Amazon

21215082R10027